RISE,

AND REIGN

Russell Walden

CONTENTS

CHAPTER ONE
Inward Conquest before Outward Victory 1

CHAPTER TWO
The Ascension Mentality 15

CHAPTER THREE
Ascend in Worship, Descend in Warfare 31

CHAPTER FOUR
Climbing Jacob's Ladder..43

CHAPTER FIVE
Locating Yourself in the Ascension....................51

CHAPTER SIX
Walking in the Entitlement of Sons....................61

CHAPTER ONE

INWARD CONQUEST BEFORE OUTWARD VICTORY

UNDERSTANDING THE AUTHORITY OF THE BELIEVER:

The authority of the believer is a subject often mentioned in popular Christian ministry but very little understood. It is used to get a lot of amends and to stir people emotionally, but at the end of the service, the people are dismissed little changed. Their lives are marked by captivity; their families are a mess. The economic Pharaohs of our day financially bind them as they go about living out lives of limitation, desperation, and lack. This fact does not go unnoticed by the religious cheerleaders who want to call their darkness light, so they take the position that the Pharisee and religious elites of Jerusalem took when Jesus challenged them on this very point in John chapter eight.

Jesus came that morning from the Mount of Olives to the temple mount. He was gathered with his disciples and had just confronted the scribes and Pharisees over the woman taken in adultery.

> *[Jhn 8:1-4 KJV] 1 Jesus went unto the mount of Olives. 2 And early in the morning he came again into the temple, and all the people came unto him, and he sat down and taught them. 3 And the scribes and Pharisees brought unto him a woman taken in adultery; and when they had set her in the midst, 4 They say unto him, Master, this woman was taken in adultery, in the very act.*

What the Pharisees and scribes saw was an offender deserving of death. What Jesus saw was a woman held captive in sin – an object of ridicule to the very class of men who took full advantage of her kind when it served their purpose and openly scorned her even threatened her life if it so pleased them. What is the difference between Jesus' viewpoint and that of the scribes and the Pharisees? They were held captive by what she represented to them, and Jesus was not tempted in the least. Have you ever asked yourself why Jesus responded so differently to the most despicable, guilty people around him when everyone else looked upon them with disdain?

> *[Rom 2:22 KJV] 22 Thou that sayest a man should not commit adultery, dost thou commit adultery? thou that abhorrest idols, dost thou, commit sacrilege?*

This is the question Jesus could well have asked these men because while they claimed to have caught the woman in the very act, the man involved was not presented to Jesus with her. Why not? Because he was one of them, one of their number. At the beginning of Romans ch. 2, the language could not be more explicit:

> *[Rom 2:1 KJV] 1 Therefore thou art inexcusable, O man, whosoever thou art that judgest: for wherein thou judgest another, thou condemnest thyself; for thou that judgest doest the same things.*

The word "judge" there means to have or to hand down an opinion. Do you have an opinion? The word heresy in the New Testament means to be opinionated to the point of division. These men had an opinion about themselves and about this woman that provoked them to draw a line of self-justification between themselves and the woman, thus confirming by Paul's statement in Rom. 2:1 above that they were guilty of the same thing. Jesus, on the other hand, had nothing but compassion for her. Solomon put it this way:

> *[Pro 27:19 KJV] 19 As in water face [answereth] to face, so the heart of man to man.*

In other words, what you see that provokes in you a response other than one that typifies the spirit of Christ answers the fact that the same thing is true of you. Case in point – when Evangelist Jimmy Swaggart said that Televangelist Jim Bakker was a cancer that needed to be cut out of the body of Christ (for adultery) what was Jimmy doing on the backside of Baton Rouge, Louisiana? The same thing. Why are we saying these things? To identify captivity in ourselves that we might understand just how desperately we need to appropriate the deliverance inherent in the authority that Christ confers upon the believer FIRST to overcome sin in themselves and then to walk as God carriers in the earth.

Jesus confronts us with our own captivity in this passage, and the temptation is to respond as those with Jesus responded.

> *[Jhn 8:31-36 KJV] 31 Then said Jesus to those Jews which believed on him, If ye continue in*

> *my word, [then] are ye, my disciples, indeed; 32 And ye shall know the truth, and the truth shall make you free. 33 They answered him, we be Abraham's seed, and were never in bondage to any man: how sayest thou, Ye shall be made free? 34 Jesus answered them, Verily, verily, I say unto you, whosoever committeth sin is the servant of sin. 35 And the servant abideth not in the house for ever: [but] the Son abideth ever. 36 If the Son, therefore, shall make you free, ye shall be free indeed.*

Notice that Jesus is not talking to the scribes and Pharisees that brought the woman taken in adultery. They had all left the scene. He is speaking to those Jews (those with a performance-based approach to God willing to justify themselves). They were Jews who believed in Jesus but Jews nonetheless. Jesus, in effect, says "not good enough..." You have to do more than demonstrate a willingness to believe – you have to abandon who you are and your own sense of self-worth by CONTINUING in the word (v. 31) to true freedom. Jesus tries to point this out, and they object saying in their words "what freedom are you talking about – we have never been in bondage to any man!" What a lie this was. They were as an entire nation living with the jackboot of Rome in their neck, but they had changed their definition of freedom to conveniently ignore the fact of their deepest captivity!

What is YOUR deepest captivity? Looking past all the compartmentalization where we are pristine and pure examples of life in Christ on the one hand and something else altogether in another part of your life that no one, not even those who know you best are aware of. You see we can jump up and down and celebrate what we think is the authority we have as believers, but until the INNER CONQUEST is accomplished, the OUTER VICTORY will never be realized.

> *[Pro 16:32 KJV] 32 [He that is] slow to anger [is] better than the mighty; and he that ruleth his spirit than he that taketh a city.*

Do you see what this is saying? There is no OUTER VICTORY until INNER CONQUEST is accomplished. Solomon is comparing this to an army besieging a city. A city has walls, gates, and defenses. When the city is brought under siege, the defenses are brought up. In Judges 9 there was a man named Abimelech who besieged a city. The gates were about to be breached, but then something happened:

> *[Jdg 9:51-53 KJV] 51 But there was a strong tower within the city, and thither fled all the men and women, and all they of the city, and shut [it] to them, and gat them up to the top of the tower. 52 And Abimelech came unto the tower, and fought against it, and went hard unto the door of the tower to burn it with fire. 53 And a certain woman cast a piece of a millstone upon Abimelech's head, and all to brake his skull.*

What do we do when someone puts us under pressure? If they throw a rock of accusation at us, we throw it back. Isn't that really what Jesus is after in this entire situation recorded in John 8. Someone says something to you that you don't like, and you form a defensive response to them usually accompanies by an accusation impugning that person's character. This demonstrates one great truth:

To the degree you level blame you establish your own guilt.

What I want you to do today is to call a truce, put down your opinions, and take a good hard look at yourself. It's called humility. Humility is the one great secret weapon of the believer. When you take the posture of humility, all of heaven opens up to come to your aid – first to conquer your inner territory and then to secure for you – your outward victory. The enemy has no defense against humility because he doesn't have any. He cannot find you when you walk in humility, and he cannot deceive you with false humility because he can't counterfeit what he doesn't understand.

How do we implement this process in ourselves that leads to such miraculous outcomes? Peter – a man whose journey to the posture of humility is fully documented in the scripture, said the following:

> *[1Pe 5:5-9 KJV] 5 Likewise, ye younger, submit yourselves unto the elder. Yea, all [of you] be subject one to another, and be clothed with humility: for God resisteth the proud, and giveth grace to the humble. 6 Humble yourselves therefore under the mighty hand of God, that he may exalt you in due time: 7 Casting all your care upon him; for he careth for you. 8 Be sober, be vigilant; because your adversary the devil, as a roaring lion, walketh about, seeking whom he may devour: 9 Whom*

> *resist steadfast in the faith, knowing that the same afflictions are accomplished in your brethren that are in the world.*

Notice that Peter didn't say humble yourself on general principles. He is very specific. He says humble yourself under the hand of God. What is the hand of God? We have four fingers on each hand and one thumb. Interesting enough, we likewise have four mentions of the finger of God in the scriptures:

> *[Exo 8:19 KJV] 19 Then the magicians said unto Pharaoh, this [is] the finger of God: and Pharaoh's heart was hardened, and he hearkened not unto them; as the LORD had said.*

Note the connection of the finger of God with the issue of humility of which Pharaoh had none. Pharaoh's heart was hardened, refusing to release the people. How many people languish under your refusal to release them from what you think they owe you? We experience the finger of God when we extend to others the compassion, we desire to experience ourselves from the heart of God.

> *[Exo 31:18 KJV] 18 And he gave unto Moses,*

> *when he had made an end of communing with him upon mount Sinai, two tables of testimony, tables of stone, written with the finger of God.*

The tablets of the testimony God gave Moses were written with the "finger of God..." This is God inscribing on your heart in the place of communion with Him those things that are non-optional in your life. We experience the finger of God in the place of communion with Him – not to define what God expects of others but what God expects of us.

> *[Deu 9:10 KJV] 10 And the LORD delivered unto me two tables of stone written with the finger of God; and on them [was written] according to all the words, which the LORD spake with you in the mount out of the midst of the fire in the day of the assembly.*

The voice of God was heard in the mountain in the midst of the fire. What is the theme we are considering? Rise – Rule – Reign? If you are going to hear from God, you are going to have to ascend unto Him. According to Paul, Moses gave us this example:

> *[Rom 10:5-7 KJV] 5 For Moses describeth the*

righteousness which is of the law, That the man which doeth those things shall live by them. 6 But the righteousness which is of faith speaketh on this wise, say not in thine heart, who shall ascend into heaven? (that is, to bring Christ down [from above] :) 7 Or, who shall descend into the deep? (that is, to bring up Christ again from the dead.)

God says, "I'm not coming down there to you – I've already done that..." We need to be careful we are not saying in our expectations that the work of the cross was not enough. What more would you have the audacity to ask Him to do what He hasn't already done on the cross? We experience the finger of God when we ascend to Him on His terms and not ours.

[Luk 11:20 KJV] 20 But if I with the finger of God cast out devils, no doubt the kingdom of God is come upon you.

Jesus describes the finger of God as that which casts out devils. John Wimber was asked, "can a Christian have a devil?" He smiled and asked in return, "Does the Christian want one?" What is the point? God will always deliver you from your enemies, but He will never deliver you from your friends. David gives us insight into this in Psalms 103:

> *[Psa 103:1 KJV] 1 [[[A Psalm] of David.]] Bless the LORD, O my soul: and all that is within me, [bless] his holy name.*

David understood there was a cacophony of discord within man that needed to be conquered and brought to heel at the foot of the cross. You will never experience outward victory until the inward conquest is fulfilled. Over and again, Jesus cast out devils and said: "go and sin no more..." The thoughts of the enemy and influence of the enemy touches your life because it finds an environment compatible with his working. It's not your wife's fault. It's not your husband's fault. You can't blame the pastor, or your boss or anyone else – as the song says, "it's ain't nobody's fault but mine..." You experience the finger of God when you take responsibility for your own captivity and receive the deliverance that God has for you.

Peter said, God, resists the proud. That means God sets His forces in array against the proud. In Proverbs 13:10, Solomon said contention only comes by pride. Is there contention in your life? Opinion? Objection? Offense? These are the predictors of downfall in your life. The clock is ticking. The fuse is lit. Destruction is imminent – but if you run to the hand of God... the fingers of the hand are likeness as well to apostle, prophet, evangelist, pastor, and teacher. If you set aside your intransigent commitment to self-determination – that isn't getting you in life where you want to go – and seek out those giftings intended to bring about the fullness of the measure of the stature of Christ – then the way is made clear for you to rise up out of self-sabotage and failure into your destiny in God.

CHAPTER TWO

THE ASCENSION MENTALITY

What we have covered so far: In chapter one of Rise, Rule, and Reign, we found out that outward rule never comes before inward victory. If you are ever going to get free and stay free in God, you have to define your own captivity. The most effective way to do that is to identify judgments you have made toward others. As face answers to face, Solomon declared, so the heart of man answers to the heart of man. When we claim to know the better path, we are confirming according to Paul that we aren't on it. From that perspective of personal self-disclosure, we can have a moment of clarity to humble ourselves – and then begin to rise, to ascend in God who always exalts the humble but resists the proud at every turn.

Another way of expressing the need for the believer to "Rise, Rule, and Reign" is to make the declaration to the believer "come up higher!" This comes from Rev. 4:1:

> *[Rev 4:1 KJV] 1 After this I looked, and, behold, a door [was] opened in heaven: and the first voice which I heard [was] as it were of a trumpet talking with me; which said, Come up hither, and I will shew thee things which must be hereafter.*

We see what this meant in John's vision, but what does it mean for us? Does it just mean for us to be encouraged? Is it just being positive in God realizing that in Christ, we have authority yet to be discovered if we will only take our minds off our problems? There is validity in this even as Moses commanded when the people were bitten by vipers:

> *[Num 21:8 KJV] 8 And the LORD said unto Moses, make thee a fiery serpent, and set it upon a pole: and it shall come to pass, that every one that is bitten when he looketh upon it, shall live.*

So "look and live." Get your eyes off your problems and look to Jesus, and things will get better. Is that all there is to "Rise, Rule, and Reign?"

Scriptures on Ascension and Ruling in Christ:

In Ephesians 2:6, Paul declares that part of being born again is something described as being seated with Christ in heavenly places:

> *[Eph 2:6 KJV] 6 And hath raised [us] up together, and made [us] sit together in heavenly [places] in Christ Jesus:*

Isn't that encouraging? Is that all that Paul is trying to do – just encouraging us – not to feel beat down or subject to the depredations and struggles of life? We read these verses, and they do make our hearts feel buoyant and encouraged but is that all there is to it? We need to find out because there may be something essential to what God has provided us that we overlooked because we are reading these passages as mere poetry rather than allowing them to inform the narrative of our life in Christ. Through the Prophet Isaiah, the Spirit of God makes a declaration that those who walk in humility will ascend and dwell in high places in God:

> *[Isa 57:15 KJV] 15 For thus saith the high and lofty One that inhabiteth eternity, whose name [is] Holy; I dwell in the high and holy [place], with him also [that is] of a contrite and*

humble spirit, to revive the spirit of the humble, and to revive the heart of the contrite ones.

Now is this literal? Does God tell everyone who is actually humble to move to Colorado and live above the tree line? If you have ever spent any time in the mountains of Colorado, you will find there are many different sorts of people in the mountains, but they don't as a people group have a monolithic testimony of their humility before God. Likewise, if we apply that verse literally to the characters in the Bible there would only be three people who by that definition would be truly humble: Jesus who ascended up on high, Elijah who went up by a fiery chariot and Enoch who walked with God and was not for God took him. The rest of us must be full of pride for we didn't make it! What is it then to have an ascension mentality and walk, live, and be seated practically speaking in heavenly places in Christ?

You Are Where Your Attention Takes You:

Science has had a hard time studying and defining what the human capability of attention is. In the book of Colossians, the Apostle Paul gave the following statement that emphasizes that you are where your attention takes you:

> *[Col 3:1-4 KJV] 1 If ye then be risen with Christ, seek those things which are above, where Christ sitteth on the right hand of God. 2 Set your affection on things above, not on things on the earth. 3 For ye are dead, and your life is hidden with Christ in God. 4 When Christ, [who is] our life, shall appear, then shall ye also appear with him in glory.*

We are risen with Christ whether we realize it in our day to day life or not. However, when we SET OUR AFFECTION (lit. emotional attenuation) upon things above, then we are dead to the world (the fallen cosmos and society), and our life is hidden with Christ in God. What life is Paul talking about that is "hid with Christ..." the word there is Zoe, and it means the God kind of life or the life of the Spirit. Now we are getting somewhere. There are three kinds of life spoken of in the scripture:

Zoe – the life of your human spirit.

Psuche – the life of your mind, will, and emotions.

Carne – the life of your flesh.

You can experience these three distinct aspects of life in unequivocal terms if you pay attention, but we are to focus, put our attention on the Zoe of God on the inside of us for it is that which is who God is inside of us. You need to understand that Zoe – the life of God inside of you is so vitally connected to who He is that theologically He is inseparable from it as the following verse demonstrates:

> *[Deu 30:20 KJV] 20 That thou mayest love the LORD thy God, [and] that thou mayest obey his voice, and that thou mayest cleave unto him: for he [is] thy life, and the length of thy days: that thou mayest dwell in the land which the LORD sware unto thy fathers, to Abraham, to Isaac, and to Jacob, to give them.*

What is the difference between walking with God in the Old Covenant and the New Covenant? It has to do with a creative transaction that took place when you accepted Jesus as your savior. You have something that even Adam in his state of innocence did not experience. Let us consider two verses:

> *[Gen 2:7 KJV] 7 And the LORD God formed man [of] the dust of the ground, and breathed into his nostrils the breath of life; and man*

became a living soul.

Now read the following verse that describes what happens when you became born again:

> *[1Co 15:45 KJV] 45 And so it is written, the first man Adam was made a living soul; the last Adam [was made] a quickening spirit.*

What God originally intended for Adam was never consummated because Adam turned away and transgressed. What Adam forsook in the fall is restored in Christ. In Adam, the seat of his consciousness was his soul (mind, will, and emotions). This is demonstrated by the simple psychology in mankind when he says things like "I think, I feel, I will..." those statements originate in the soul because that is who Adam is. He is a soul man. In Christ, however, something different is expressed, and the life of Jesus and his own internal dialog makes this plain:

> *[Jhn 12:27 KJV] 27 Now is my soul troubled; and what shall I say? Father, save me from this hour: but for this cause came I unto this hour.*

Jesus was not saying this from His soul because

that was not where His identity – His comprehension and experience of Himself originated. He was a spirit man; thus He referred to His soul (mind, will, emotions) in the third person as we likewise refer to our body (my arm, my leg, my head, etc.). This is what the ascension mentality looks like – the seat of your identity, your comprehension of yourself moving from the soul man and the passions of sins into the spirit man where God lives and you become one with the Father.

Is this just a theological curiosity because I needed something to write down or say to you? No – it is seen to be absolutely vital as revealed in the words of Solomon in Ecclesiastes 12 speaking of the end of life as he understood it by the inspiration of the Holy Spirit:

> *[Ecc 12:6-7 KJV] 6 Or ever the silver cord be loosed, or the golden bowl be broken, or the pitcher be broken at the fountain, or the wheel broken at the cistern. 7 Then shall the dust return to the earth as it was: and the spirit shall return unto God who gave it.*

There is a silver cord or a divine connection between God and man that causes a man to draw breath and his heart to beat until the appointed time when the breath of God, the spirit of man returns to God that gave it. Jesus as a man experienced life from within that part of His being which is why in John 12:27 he spoke of his soul in the third person because He knew Himself and experienced Himself as being more than the mind, will or emotions. What about you? Are you a spirit man or a soul man? More than just in your profession – but in reality. Just because you say it doesn't make it so – this is a matter of spiritual growth. Before Jesus came when men died, they either went to Sheol or Paradise depending on the character of their lives and their disposition before God. That was a very important distinction because Jesus only preached the gospel and brought release to those in Paradise between the time of His death and His resurrection.

> *[1Pe 3:18-19 KJV] 18 For Christ also hath once suffered for sins, the just for the unjust, that he might bring us to God, being put to death in the flesh, but quickened by the Spirit: 19 By which also he went and preached unto the spirits in prison;*

What is different now? After the resurrection, those who die in faith do not go to a holding place any longer – according to the Apostle Paul:

> *[1Co 5:3 KJV] 3 For I verily, as absent in body, but present in spirit, have judged already, as though I were present, [concerning] him that hath so done this deed,*

Why is this so? The letter to the Ephesians informs us:

> *[Eph 2:14 KJV] 14 For he is our peace, who hath made both one, and hath broken down the middle wall of partition [between us];*

What is the wall of partition? It is more than speaking of the racial distinction between the Jew and the Gentile nations. When David gave God his profound contrition over the matter with Bathsheba, he made some telling statements that resonate right down to our day and the work of Christ on the Cross:

> *[Psa 51:5-6 KJV] 5 Behold, I was shapen in iniquity; and in sin did my mother conceive me. 6 Behold, thou desirest truth in the inward parts: and in the hidden [part] thou shalt make me to know wisdom.*

When David says, he was shapen in iniquity that word means that he was born IMPRISONED and cut off from God. Where was God? In the heavens only? No, because Deut. 30:20 says God is your life. That is more than a poetic turn of phrase. Job put it this way:

> *[Job 27:2-3 KJV] 2 [As] God liveth, [who] hath taken away my judgment; and the Almighty, [who] hath vexed my soul; 3 All the while my breath [is] in me, and the spirit of God [is] in my nostrils;*

Job's understanding codified as a doctrine for us in the canon of scripture is that the SPIRIT of GOD and the BREATH OF LIFE are one and the same thing. Your life (what makes your heartbeat and your lungs to breath – the germ or spark of life in you) is an extension of the uncreated life of God, BUT because of sin you could not become ONE with the Father until JESUS CAME and removed the prison bars, the barrier that David lamented over in Psalm 51:5 and that Paul referred to as the PARTITION (between you and God – IN YOURSELF, within your being) that is REMOVED by the work of Christ on the Cross.

You see, you cannot ASCEND until you KNOW THE WAY and what did Jesus say in John 14:

> *[Jhn 14:6 KJV] 6 Jesus saith unto him, I am the way, the truth, and the life: no man cometh unto the Father, but by me.*

What way is Jesus? Does this mean He is the lifestyle or the methodology or personal philosophy of the believer? Much more than this. Look more closely at the words of David:

> *[Psa 51:5-6 KJV] 5 Behold, I was shapen in iniquity; and in sin did my mother conceive me. 6 Behold, thou desirest truth in the inward parts: and in the hidden [part] thou shalt make me to know wisdom.*

David speaks prophetically of God so acting upon you in your inner man BECAUSE it is the DESIRE (and plan) of God that we would know TRUTH in our INWARD PARTS (our innermost being) and be made to know WISDOM. John 14:6 already establishes for us that our TRUTH is not a creed or a doctrine but a PERSON whose name is Jesus and 1 Cor. 1:30 declares that Jesus in His person is our WISDOM.

> *[1Co 1:30 KJV] 30 But of him are ye in Christ Jesus, who of God is made unto us wisdom, and righteousness, and sanctification, and redemption:*

So in Psalm 51:5-6 David is feeling after as sense that there is something inside of himself that he understood was a HIDDEN PART of his makeup where one day that which was barred to him in a sin state would be thrown open making FULL FELLOWSHIP WITH GOD once again possible by the work of Christ upon the Cross – which could not be preached until Jesus paid the price but as soon as Jesus paid for the sin that necessitated the imprisonment of man away from God – now the way is made clear and He showed up where the Old Testament saints could be found and Eph. 4:8 says:

> *[Eph 4:8 KJV] 8 Wherefore he saith, when he ascended up on high, he led captivity captive and gave gifts unto men.*

What are the gifts? The gifts of the Holy Spirit. The gifts of the callings and anointings that man could not carry until the sin debt was paid and the prison doors were open making possible for a man to be indwelled of God for God to be in US and for US to be in God - - with implications far-reaching beyond what we could even exaggerate.

CONCLUSION:

I want you to understand what it means to ascend or to RISE. This is more than a theme of a conference; it is a holy aspiration commended to us by the Apostle Paul:

> *[Col 3:1 KJV] 1 If ye then be risen with Christ, seek those things which are above, where Christ sitteth on the right hand of God.*

The resurrection Paul is referring to here is not life after death because it is spoken of in the past tense. If you are RISEN with CHRIST – as the way has been made open, the middle wall of partition Paul spoke of and David referred to it is now possible for you to ascend from the bondage of the SOUL LIFE (will, mind, emotions) to experientially (not just conceptually as a doctrine) to become ONE WITH THE FATHER and such a potentiality is the deepest longing of the heart of God and the centerpiece of the work of redemption:

> *[Jhn 4:23-24 KJV] 23 But the hour cometh, and now is, when the true worshippers shall worship the Father in spirit and in truth: for the Father seeketh such to worship him. 24 God [is] a Spirit: and they that worship him must worship [him] in spirit and in truth.*

When Jesus spoke of worshipping God in spirit and in truth that was not a turn of phrase He used only as to say God wants us to worship Him in sincerity. No Jesus is referring to the forensic reality – the experiential, transformational vortex of what becomes possible when you accept Jesus as savior. To move your sense of self and identify from the SOUL (mind, will emotion) into the Spirit where God lives. This is referred to as death working in you, but life manifesting in Christ. What does that mean? Death is separation. When the spirit leaves the body – death results, likewise, you have been brought to the death of the Cross when your sense of self – your identify moves from the limitations and parameters of your SOUL into the limitlessness of your SPIRIT and THE SOUL DIES because it has been separated from that which never should have been bound there in the first place! You were created to be one with God, not one with your SELF (psuche/soul). In Christ, in the new creation, the self-consciousness that cast Adam into darkness because of sin in Christ is once more eclipsed by the light of God. The self-consciousness goes into outer darkness to face its judgment and God-consciousness once more reigns on the inside of you.

This is the progression of Spiritual Maturity that ought to take place after your new birth, but it doesn't because you haven't been taught what Paul admonished the Galatians:

> *[Gal 5:25 KJV] 25 If we live in the Spirit, let us also walk in the Spirit.*

If we are going to walk in the Spirit – WHERE ARE WE GOING TO GO? Jesus tells us in John 16:10 and 16:16 when He said, "I go to the Father..." and what He promised in John 14:

> *[Jhn 14:1-4 KJV] 1 Let not your heart be troubled: ye believe in God, believe also in me. 2 In my Father's house are many mansions: if [it were] not [so], I would have told you. I go to prepare a place for you. 3 And if I go and prepare a place for you, I will come again, and receive you unto myself; that where I am, [there] ye may be also. 4 And whither I go ye know, and the way ye know.*

So, are you a SOUL MAN or a SPIRIT MAN? One day your spirit – the breath of life will go back to God that gave it. Back to the God that Hebrews 12:29 says is a CONSUMING FIRE. For those that are wrapped up in the SOUL that will be hell. For those that have walked out of the soul realm into spiritual habitation with Christ not just as a concept but as a reality that will be HEAVEN. Make heaven your home TODAY, and it will be no big change when your body goes there at the end of your earth walk. This is the ascension mentality.

CHAPTER THREE

ASCEND IN WORSHIP, DESCEND IN WARFARE

Remember that these things are line upon line building into our thinking an ascension mentality. With that thought, let us review: In chapter one of Rise, Rule, and Reign, we found out that inward victory must come before outward rule. Solomon declared:

> *[Pro 16:32 KJV] 32 [He that is] slow to anger [is] better than the mighty; and he that ruleth his spirit than he that taketh a city.*

The things that make you angry reflect your own captivity. Prov. 27:19 tells us:

> *[Pro 27:19 KJV] 19 As in water face [answereth] to face, so the heart of man to man.*

The judgment you make against others is merely a reflection of your own shortcomings and bitter root resentments. That is why you must forgive and walk in love before faith works to move your mountain (Gal. 5:6).

In chapter two, we found that only our spirit can ascend to God (Ecc. 12:7), which is why Jesus declared in John 4:23:

> *[Jhn 4:23 KJV] 23 But the hour cometh, and now is, when the true worshippers shall worship the Father in spirit and in truth: for the Father seeketh such to worship him.*

What this means is that your sense of self-referral must move out of the soul man and into the realm of the Spirit because only your human spirit can tread his courts. Your human spirit is created from the inbreathing of God's created spirit (Job 27:3). One day God will inhale back into Himself what He exhaled into you that made you a living soul. One day born-again or no, you will go back to God that Hebrews 12:29 tells us is a consuming fire. For the sinner that will be hell. For the believer, it will be the consummation of all you have been pursuing in God your whole life.

In this portion, we will learn that we must ascend in worship if we are ever going to descend in warfare. When Jesus said in John 4:23

that the Father was seeking such to worship Him, he was talking about a whole lot more than electric guitars, cute girls, and smoke machines on Sunday morning. What we do with music and song is not worship; it is only the expression of worship. We hardly know what the word worship means. Let's look at it together. The word that Jesus used for worship in John 4 includes the following variations of meaning:

1. To kiss the hand.
2. To prostrate one's self.
3. To fall on your knees and touch the ground with your forehead.
4. To do homage.
5. To make obeisance.
6. To show respect or make supplication to those of higher rank.

There is something in American culture that recoils to see someone kiss someone's hand or kneel before them unless it is in a romantic context. That tells us that our western ideations of love are not love; they are worship. If a man kneels before a woman, she expects a ring – a covenant of agreement. If a man kisses her hand, he is a gentleman, but what is really going on? We need to be careful lest we look for in romantic love what can only be found in relationship to God alone – because that would be idolatry.

How do we worship him, and the expression not be anything other than a hollow, empty show? Evan Roberts of the Welsh Revival gave us a profound example when at the beginning of that outpouring his singular prayer was BEND US OH, GOD. BEND US TO THY WILL AND SAVE THE WORLD ... and virtually the whole of the nation of Wales came to know Jesus as their savior.

JESUS SAID IN THE GOSPEL OF MATTHEW:

[Mat 4:19 KJV] 19 And he saith unto them, follow me, and I will make you.

When a red-blooded American hears that their reflexive response is "nobody is going to MAKE me do ANYTHING!" Because we have confused LIBERTY with LICENSE. In my generation, the very definition of turning 18 was to reach the age where no one could tell you what to do anymore. That is the very opposite of worship.

If you are going to ascend, you will do so only in humility. Solomon said:

> *[Pro 16:18 KJV] 18 Pride [goeth] before destruction, and an haughty spirit before a fall.*

If pride brings us down, then it follows that HUMILITY brings us up, causes us to ascend into God. That is interesting because the word humility in the Bible is literally defined: "to go low..." So – the way UP is DOWN. It's the UPSIDE-DOWN KINGDOM.

You go low to ascend in worship and then descend in warfare with the armament that the king has equipped you with to defeat your enemy — first the inward giants and then the outward mountains.

You might say, "I have been humbled... you don't know what I've been through..."

Here is a great test of determining pride or humility:

> *[Pro 13:10 KJV] 10 Only by pride cometh contention: but with the well-advised [is] wisdom.*

I wish it said pride only comes with contention unless you are in the right, but that isn't what it means. If you are in dispute, you are in pride.

James declared:

> *[Jas 3:16 KJV] 16 For where envying and strife [is], there [is] confusion and every evil work.*

Where there is contention, there is pride, confusion, and every evil work. Now you might say – that's right I'm in contention with my pastor so he must be in pride – no you aren't in contention you are in rebellion and 1 Sam. 15:23 tells us:

> *[1Sa 15:23 KJV] 23 For rebellion [is as] the sin of witchcraft, and stubbornness [is as] iniquity and idolatry. Because thou hast rejected the word of the LORD, he hath also rejected thee from [being] king.*

Now if we ascend in worship and worship is more than instruments and music where do we start? Go to Gen. 28:

> *[Gen 28:10-13 KJV] 10 And Jacob went out from Beersheba, and went toward Haran. 11 And he lighted upon a certain place, and tarried there all night, because the sun was set, and he took of the stones of that place, and put [them for] his pillows, and lay down in*

> *that place to sleep. 12 And he dreamed, and behold a ladder set up on the earth, and the top of it reached to heaven: and behold the angels of God ascending and descending on it. 13 And, behold, the LORD stood above it, and said, I [am] the LORD God of Abraham thy father, and the God of Isaac: the land whereon thou liest, to thee will I give it, and to thy seed;*

Are you ready for God to give you the land? Then you better find the ladder that He is standing above waiting for you to look up. Where is that ladder? It is found stored in Isa. 11:2:

> *[Isa 11:2 KJV] 2 And the spirit of the LORD shall rest upon him, the spirit of wisdom and understanding, the spirit of counsel and might, the spirit of knowledge and of the fear of the LORD;*

How do we know there is a ladder here? Because there is a beginning and an ending. The beginning point is the fear of the Lord because Psalm 111:10 tells us:

> *[Psa 111:10 KJV] 10 The fear of the LORD [is] the beginning of wisdom: a good*

understanding have all they that do [his commandments]: his praise endureth forever.

So, there is our bottom rung. If you look at the TOP of that LADDER, the top rung is the Spirit of the Lord Himself who once we approach that ascension point – that portal He stands above it and pronounces our possession of the land that He has accorded us. This is the TRUE PORTAL the ONLY PORTAL you will EVER find in God, and it is on the inside of you in that place in your character and makeup reserved for HUMILITY. Now – is it vacant or is it populated?

1. So, the Fear of the Lord is first.
2. Knowledge. When the fear of the Lord came, you were prepared for the saving KNOWLEDGE brought to you by the preacher who preached the word (Rom. 10:14).
3. Might. Now – when the fear of the Lord, knowledge – knowledge or GNOSIS of God causes you to be strong and do exploits (Dan. 11:32). Most Christians never get this far.
4. Counsel. When the fear of the Lord motivates you and knowledge informs you strength comes to take action. That is

when you have to iron some things out in the counsel of God.
5. Understanding. After you received the counsel of God, your understanding was opened, and you began to see things differently. You are in an environment alien to faith. You are a warrior, and you need marching orders now.
6. Then the Spirit of Wisdom (1 Cor. 1:30) Jesus is your wisdom. Wisdom tells you what to do with the knowledge, understanding, and might that now characterize your life in God.
7. Spirit of the Lord: When wisdom comes, God reacts because 1 Cor. 1:30 tells us Jesus is your wisdom. When the Spirit of Wisdom drops on you – the Father thinks you look just like Jesus and grants the whole of the kingdom with its authority and prerogatives into your lap and suddenly everything you say and do becomes as effective as if God said it and did it.

This is the process of ascending in worship that brings about the outcome of descending in warfare and putting your foot in the enemy's neck – first IN yourself and then in the environment around you. Then you are a king under the King of Kings ruling and reigning upon the earth as Paul insisted 2 Tim. 2:12:

> [2Ti 2:12 KJV] 12 If we suffer, we shall also reign with [him]: if we deny [him], he also will deny us:

What is the suffering? It is the process that gets us to Bethel like Jacob. Jacob was on the run. He didn't try to fight his own battles. His Father said go, and he went and where that led him was into the experience that opened the entitlements of heaven by the word of the one standing at the top of that ladder declaring COVENANTAL ENTITLEMENT OVER HIS LIFE.

So, where are you? Are you still trying to con your brother out of the birthright like Jacob? Or are you still trying to deceive God by fixing yourself up like venison stew into what you think He will respond to? Or are you on the run from an Esau who is seeking your life? Or are you at Bethel were true ascension begins? The process is yours to walk out, but the end result is reflected in:

> [Isa 57:15 KJV] 15 For thus saith the high and lofty One that inhabiteth eternity, whose name

> *[is] Holy; I dwell in the high and holy [place], with him also [that is] of a contrite and humble spirit, to revive the spirit of the humble, and to revive the heart of the contrite ones.*

When Jacob stood in his dream at the bottom of that ladder that angels ascended and descended upon – He saw God Himself standing above it making declaration over His life:

> *Gen. 28:13 And, behold, the LORD stood above it, and said, I [am] the LORD God of Abraham thy father, and the God of Isaac: the land whereon thou liest, to thee will I give it, and to thy seed;*

This is the same ladder that Jesus told Nathaniel he would experience in seeing the angels of heaven ascending and descending upon the Son of Man of which He is the head, and you and I are the many-membered body. What are the angels doing? They are carrying out the implementation of the dictates of the New Covenant on your behalf.

CHAPTER FOUR

CLIMBING JACOB'S LADDER

What have we covered so far in chapters one through three? In chapter one of Rise, Rule, and Reign, we learned that there is no lasting outward victory without inward conquest.

> *[Pro 16:32 KJV] 32 [He that is] slow to anger [is] better than the mighty; and he that ruleth his spirit than he that taketh a city.*

In chapter two, we discovered the Ascension Mentality. If ever you are going to experience kingdom authority in your life, you must vacate the convenience of your soul and live out of your spirit as Jesus did. The soul is dependent on the body and its natural environment. You cannot rule over that which you are dependent on. Jesus didn't need the natural realm; rather, the natural realm needed him; therefore, He bent it to His will. He walked on water. He walked through walls. He made human eyes from nothing more than spit and clay. He did all this from a posture of being ONE with His Father who lives in the human spirit and seeks those to worship Him not in the natural realm or the soul realm of the emotions but in Spirit and in Truth. Who is the Truth? Jesus is the Truth, and if you are going to be IN Him, you are going to have to move out of the soul realm and take up residence, centering yourself in the human spirit that He has provided for you to have fellowship and relationship with Him.

In chapter three, we ascended in worship in order to descend in warfare. Humility is the great secret weapon of the saints. Through humility we find ourselves at the beginning of wisdom which is the fear of the Lord – the first of the seven spirits of God by which we ascend into a ratified covenant by which God certifies the availability of an experience and walk with Him where everything you say and do becomes as effective as if He said it and did it.

CLIMBING JACOBS LADDER:

In the last chapter, we concluded standing side by side with Jacob looking up that ladder that represented the seven spirits of God. Every one of those seven spirits of God operates in your life at some time or another. If you listen with the ear of the spirit you will discern your season and discerning your season will make all the difference in what happens next in your life. If you are on the bottom rung that corresponds to the Spirit of the Fear of the Lord. That is a season to walk circumspectly not as a fool:

> [Eph 5:15-17 KJV] 15 See then that ye walk circumspectly, not as fools, but as wise, 16 Redeeming the time, because the days are evil. 17 Wherefore be ye not unwise, but understanding what the will of the Lord [is].

The word, according to Hebrews 4:12, is the great discerner.

> [Heb 4:12 KJV] 12 For the word of God [is] quick, and powerful, and sharper than any two-edged sword, piercing even to the dividing asunder of soul and spirit, and of the joints and marrow, and [is] a discerner of the thoughts and intents of the heart.

You don't have to look at the situation, you only have to look at God and see what He is doing, and you will understand what is happening around you. When the Spirit of the Fear of the Lord is on you, it is because the days are evil.

Circumstances are out there, and you don't want to take anything for granted. When we align with the heart of God at that point, it opens the door of advancement, and you RISE to:

The Spirit of knowledge. Why do we need knowledge? Because if the days are evil, you need protection and provision. The knowledge of God provides these according to 2 Peter 1:3:

> *[2Pe 1:3 KJV] 3 According as his divine power hath given unto us all things that [pertain] unto life and godliness, through the knowledge of him that hath called us to glory and virtue:*

Do you lack anything? Stop asking God for jelly beans from heaven. Go find the Spirit of the fear of the Lord and align with that and promotion will come that brings the knowledge of God online to provide ALL THINGS (all means all leaving nothing out). What is this? Knowledge of some conspiracy theory? Knowledge of the secret Illuminati plot to overthrow society and bring in the New World Order? No! That knowledge doesn't do you ANY GOOD but the KNOWLEDGE of the Lord – the "knowledge of Him" as Peter declares will give you all things that pertain to life (your situation) and godliness (your destiny) and open you up to the glory and virtue that characterizes the next spirit of God on His ascension ladder of Isaiah 11:1-3.

We all want to move in the MIGHT of God and the COUNSELS of HEAVEN, but if there is no fear of God in your eyes and no knowledge of God in your heart the COUNSELS OF HEAVEN are against you, and the might of God would destroy you because you wouldn't know how to handle it. This is God's way, and Jesus said in John 10:1 if you try to climb up another way you are aligning yourself with thieves and robbers. So many people want the power of God and plan of God and the might of God, but they want it to come with a dollop of glory in a moment of time without any process by which they are transformed and changed into God's image. They want outward shift without inward transformation, and that isn't God's way. It is in line with Charismatic and Pentecostal theology but not in line with the heart of God.

After the fear of God secures you and the knowledge of God informs you, then you will fulfill Daniel 11:32:

> [Dan 11:32 KJV] 32 And such as do wickedly against the covenant shall he corrupt by flatteries: but the people that do know their

God shall be strong, and do [exploits].

You won't do wickedly against the Covenant. What covenant? The one that God made with Jacob standing above the ladder that we are talking about here. You won't be corrupted by flattery because you know the angels of heaven are ascending and descending upon your life. Now you begin to UNDERSTAND some things about God, and you start to walk in the WISDOM of God and let the WISDOM OF GOD walk around in you.

The next Spirit of God is the Spirit of UNDERSTANDING. Understanding isn't the top of the ladder; it is only one step along the way. People clamor for understanding and ask "why God," but understanding is highly over-rated. It is just something you pass by on your way to ascension in Him. People who only want to understand will stop half-way, and the only thing they will accomplish is impeding everyone who comes after them. Understanding won't take you to the top of God's ladder. You have to follow the peace that Paul spoke of:

> *[Phl 4:7 KJV] 7 And the peace of God, which passeth all understanding, shall keep your hearts and minds through Christ Jesus.*

When Paul tried to understand he was killing Christians. Then He had an encounter with WISDOM on the road to Damascus:

> *[Act 9:3-4 KJV] 3 And as he journeyed, he came near Damascus: and suddenly there shined round about him a light from heaven: 4 And he fell to the earth, and heard a voice saying unto him, Saul, Saul, why persecutest thou me?*

Saul fell to the ground – just like Jacob and looking up it was WISDOM PERSONIFIED according to 1 Cor. 1:30 that clarified Saul's understanding and showed him what was really going on. How many of us are just like that? In ignorance, standing in opposition to the very God, we claim to serve. We are like "Wrong Way" Roy Riegels in the 1927 Rose Bowl. He has the unenviable distinction for the worst blunder in the history of college football. Halfway through the 2nd quarter he was thirty yards from a touchdown but got turned around and ran 69 yards to the wrong goalposts. They were screaming for him to stop, but it was too late. He had understanding. He knew to run with the ball, but he didn't have the wisdom to run the right direction.

When you allow wisdom to inhabit your life and your heart, there comes a rest for you because the Spirit of the Lord can now, according to v. 2 of Isaiah 11 rest on you. The Spirit of the Lord is the highest manifestation of the seven Spirits of God. When you reach there – you are at one with the Father. Everything you say and do becomes as effective as if He said it and did it. You become Lord of your Own Harvest. The seeds you sow produce a crop before they even hit the ground and the enemy can't touch you because you have stepped out of his realm of ignorance, presumption, and compromise into the full entitlement of a true son of God.

CHAPTER FIVE

LOCATING YOURSELF IN THE ASCENSION

L et's review the foundation we've laid and then delve into how to locate yourself in the ascension of God: In chapter one of Rise, Rule, and Reign, we discovered that there is no outward victory without inward conquest.

> *[Pro 16:32 KJV] 32 [He that is] slow to anger [is] better than the mighty; and he that ruleth his spirit than he that taketh a city.*

In chapter two, we discovered the Ascension Mentality. Jesus taught us that those that worship Him must do so in spirit and in truth. If you are going to worship in Spirit, you must be in the spirit. The tabernacle of Moses had three partitions – the outer court, the inner court, and the Holy of Holies. The outer court is the physical body. When night falls in that realm, you are in outer darkness. You have to anchor your experience of God on more than goosebumps or esoteric physical sensations. The inner court is where the Lamp, Table, and Altar of incense are found. This is the soul realm, and if you stop there, all you have is religion. You must move on – centering yourself and anchoring your sense of self-referral in the Holy of Holies where is found Aaron's rod that budded, the tables of the Law speaking of the Conscience, and the golden pot of Manna which represents Christ. Here the only light is the Shekinah weightiness of God's glory, and here you live and move and have your being. In chapter three, we ascended in worship in order to descend in warfare. Humility is the great secret weapon of the saints.

You never walk in greater authority than in meekness and humility. Moses was the meekest person in the earth, and when he fell on his face before God, the earth opened up and swallowed his enemies – they very definitely were "occupied elsewhere!" In chapter four, we stood with Jacob in his dream, looking up at the ladder that the angels were ascending and descending on. That ladder has seven rungs corresponding to the seven spirits of God. This is the ladder that Jesus made reference to regarding Nathaniel who like Jacob saw the angels ascending and descending upon the son of man. You might ask, how do I know this? When you see this ladder, you will know it too. These things are spiritually apprehended. If you are going to RISE that you might RULE and REIGN, you are going to have to have the artifice or at least the understanding of the artifice by which the Father shows us the way, and that is found in Isaiah 11:1-3 revealing the seven spirits of God. Once you appropriate the ascension by experience and not just doctrine – RULING and REIGNING – become a foregone conclusion.

In this portion, we will help you understand how to locate yourself in the ascension journey that God has for you and not only how to discern your season in God but how to set your season in God. Every believer will experience one of the seven spirits of God more strongly in his life at certain times. When you know for instance that the Spirit of the Fear of God is working in your life right now you know what God expects, and you know what comes next – the Spirit of Knowledge and after that the Spirit of Might, and so on. Jacob's dream about the ladder was not just for him; it is for us because, by faith, we were in him as spiritual heirs of what Jacob passed down to us from Abraham. The seven spirits of God of Isa. 11:1-3 are not just for the Old Testament because Paul said in his first letter to the Corinthians that all of the activity and work of God in the Old Testament was a coded message in metaphor, type and shadow to us in the New Testament time:

> *[1Co 10:11 KJV] 11 Now all these things happened unto them for ensamples: and they are written for our admonition, upon whom the ends of the world are come.*

Locating Yourself in God's Anointed Process:

At any given point in your life, one of the seven spirits of God will be emphasized more prominently than the others. By this Isa. 11:1-3 becomes the great discerning that locates you in your walk with God. If you are at the Spirit of the Fear of the Lord, then you are at the beginning. The Fear of the Lord is a Spirit, and fear of other things is also a spirit. Paul told Timothy:

> *[2Ti 1:7 KJV] 7 For God hath not given us the spirit of fear, but of power, and of love, and of a sound mind.*

The fear of the Lord is clean – the fear of anything else is unclean, and you can see this operating in people's lives. They fear to get older, so they do everything they can to distract themselves and others from the chronology that is manifesting in their lives. They fear a loss of a relationship and resort to every form of manipulation to hold people in their lives bound to their will. They fear losing out financially and will rob God and break every covenant of fidelity in their life to maintain their lifestyle.

Where are you at on God's ladder?

The Spirit of the Fear of the Lord

The Spirit of Knowledge

The Spirit of Might

The Spirit of Counsel

The Spirit of Understanding

The Spirit of Wisdom

The Spirit of the Lord (Himself)

Notice that the Spirit of Wisdom is just under the Spirit of the Lord Himself – 1 Cor. 1:30 says that Jesus is our wisdom and as such, He is at the right hand of the Lord even in Isa. 11:1-3. Notice also that Wisdom is the sixth Spirit revealed from man's perspective. The number 6 is the number of man, and Jesus declared that He was the son of Man. The Hebrew glyph for the number 6 is that of a tent stake, revealing Jesus is the lynchpin the point where heaven and earth come together. You cannot go around Jesus (wisdom) to get to God. Jesus said in the gospel of John:

> *[Jhn 14:6 KJV] 6 Jesus saith unto him, I am the way, the truth, and the life: no man cometh unto the Father, but by me.*

What rung are you on? What Spirit of the Seven Spirits of God is being emphasized in your life.

DISCERNING YOUR SEASON

Fear of the Lord:

Not only can you locate yourself in your walk with God by discerning which of the seven spirits is working strongest in your life – you can also discern your season. When the fear of the Lord attends our life, we don't want to make a move without Him. We are walking circumspectly, which means "barefoot" before God, as Paul said in Ephesians:

> *[Eph 5:15-16 KJV] 15 See then that ye walk*

circumspectly, not as fools, but as wise, 16 Redeeming the time, because the days are evil.

Why are we walking circumspectly? Because the days are evil. When the fear of the Lord grips your spirit, it tells you something about you, and it tells you something about what is going on around you whether you know it or not.

SPIRIT OF KNOWLEDGE

When the Spirit of Knowledge flows in your life, you learn something about yourself, and you learn something about the season you are in. The season that accompanies the Spirit of Knowledge from God is one that brings God's delivering hand and supernatural protection and preservation:

> *[Pro 2:10-11 KJV] 10 When wisdom entereth into thine heart, and knowledge is pleasant unto thy soul; 11 Discretion shall preserve thee, understanding shall keep thee:*

This is the power of the ministry of the teacher when he is sent into your midst to fill with the knowledge of God that 2 Peter 1:3 tells you will supply ALL THINGS that are lacking in your life:

[2Pe 1:3 KJV] 3 According as his divine power hath given unto us all things that [pertain] unto life and godliness, through the knowledge of him that hath called us to glory and virtue:

When the teacher comes – tell your family, "get ready to get blessed!" Get ready for the supply of God to find you and fund you for the journey ahead.

ANTICIPATING WHAT COMES NEXT:

When you know what season you are in, you know what comes next. After the fear of the Lord comes the knowledge of God, after knowledge comes might and so on. When you encounter the wisdom of God according to 1 Cor. 1:30, you know that foundations are being laid and something is being built.

[Pro 9:1 KJV] 1 Wisdom hath builded her house, she hath hewn out her seven pillars:

What are the seven pillars? The seven pillars are the seven spirits of God that go from being something you are traversing in your walk with God in terms of visitation and maturing in Him, but they become PILLARS INSTALLED IN WHO YOU ARE IN GOD. This is what John was referring to in John 3:34:

> *[Jhn 3:34 KJV] 34 For he whom God hath sent speaketh the words of God: for God giveth not the Spirit by measure [unto him].*

Are you ready for the Spirit without measure? We've been told that is only for Jesus, but there is no scripture in the Bible that even implies this.

CONCLUSION:

When the full spectrum of the Seven Spirits of God is experienced by you, they will become installed in you to be activated according to your need. Then you will experience ruling and reigning because according to John 3:34 when the spirit operates in you without measure the words that come out of your mouth are not your words, but instead, they are the words of God and no word from God ever falls to the ground. That means you will say a thing, and it will manifest. You will decree a thing, and it will rise up from the earth fully formed. You will only do what you see the Father do and only speak what you hear the Father speak and only decide according to what He breathes into your heart and mind. This is not only possible it is available as the promise of God poured out on the day of Pentecost by virtue of His holy Spirit – His seven-fold Holy Spirit if we will just cooperate and move with wisdom and understanding into all that God has for you.

CHAPTER SIX

WALKING IN THE ENTITLEMENT OF SONS

Let's sum things up thus far leading to this our final chapter: In chapter one of Rise, Rule, and Reign, we see that there is no outward triumph without inward conquest. This is what Solomon affirmed in Proverbs 16:32:

> *[Pro 16:32 KJV] 32 [He that is] slow to anger [is] better than the mighty; and he that ruleth his spirit than he that taketh a city.*

If you want to take your city for God, you must conquer that unexplored, unrestrained inner territory first. If you think the cross took care of it all, you better think again. When Joshua went into the Promised Land, God left the giants and the Canaanites in the land for the people of God to overcome as they took their possession. Your inner Canaanite must be defeated before the walls of your personal Jericho will fall. Each of the mountains and peoples that Joshua conquered speaks directly to an aspect of conquest that must take place in your inner life before outward reigning can take place.

In chapter two, we adopted the Ascension Mentality where our goal is that our sense of self transitions from the soul ("I think, I will, I feel) to the spirit where God lives. Then we can say with Jesus in John 5:19, "I only do what I see the Father do." You make your decisions based on the Father's judgments and not your own (John 5:30); and you speak not of yourself (John 12:49) but only what the Father in your spirit gives you to speak. In chapter three, we ascended in worship in order to descend in warfare. Humility is the great secret weapon of the saints. In chapter four, we learned about Jacob's ladder and the seven spirits of God. If you are going to ascend you need a ladder and it is stored in Isaiah 11:2:

> *[Isa 11:2 KJV] 2 And the spirit of the LORD shall rest upon him, the spirit of wisdom and understanding, the spirit of counsel and might, the spirit of knowledge and the fear of the LORD;*

Finally, in chapter five we showed in understanding the ascension process revealed in the seven spirits of God you then know how to locate yourself in God's process (how to identify the season you are in) and at the same time know what comes next. If the Spirit of the fear of the Lord is operating in your life, you know it is a time to walk circumspectly before God. You also know that the next season will be one where the Spirit of the Knowledge of the Lord will come as the Teacher to teach you something important. Why is that necessary to know? Because Peter said in 2 Peter 1:3-4 that through knowledge, God gives us all things that pertain unto life and godliness.

> *[2Pe 1:2-4 KJV] 2 Grace and peace be multiplied unto you through the knowledge of God… 3 According as his divine power hath given unto us all things that [pertain] unto life and godliness, through the knowledge of … 4 Whereby are given unto us exceeding great and precious promises: that by these ye might be partakers of the divine nature…*

This is how God answers prayer. When something is lacking in godliness or in the needs of your life God responds by adjusting your attitude through the Spirit of the Fear of the Lord and then bringing His revelation knowledge online to see to it that you obtain the great and precious promises and move into what Peter calls in 2 Peter 1 the place where you never fall and never fail.

In this portion, we will help you understand how to locate yourself in the ascension journey that God has for you and not only how to discern your season in God but how to set your season in God. This is what it means to rise, rule, and reign. You RISE UP from the worldly earthly perspective and determine that you are in pursuit of all God has for you. You encounter your unsanctified flesh, and by God's anointed process, you come to a place of RULE over your inner territory. Then and only then can you RULE in Christ. This is not something you have to wait to die to experience. Paul declared that ruling and reigning is a NOW proposition for the believer:

> *[Rom 5:17 KJV] 17 For if by one man's offence death reigned by one; much more they which receive abundance of grace and of the gift of righteousness shall reign in life by one, Jesus Christ.)*

Ruling and reigning begins now. You don't have to die to rule and reign with Christ. What is this fascination with death Christians have? They think after they die they will understand it better "bye and bye." They believe after death all answers will come, and then they will be in Christ and rule with Him in a fashion that theologians insist only begins after we depart this life. Show me in the scripture where that is true. Remember the words of Paul in 1 Cor. 15:

> *[1Co 15:26 KJV] 26 The last enemy [that] shall be destroyed [is] death.*

Religious mentality says after we die we will be perfect. Why would God use His final enemy to accomplish His purpose? Note that Paul said in Rom. 5:17 that the believer reigns IN LIFE by one Christ Jesus. He didn't say that we reign AFTER DEATH. Let's come into agreement with God.

What does ruling and reigning look like in this life? This is not a minor theme in the scriptures:

> *[Rev 1:6 KJV] 6 And hath made us kings and priests unto God and his Father; to him [be] glory and dominion for ever and ever. Amen.*

> *[Rev 5:10 KJV] 10 And hast made us unto our God kings and priests: and we shall reign on the earth.*

> *[1Pe 2:9 KJV] 9 But ye [are] a chosen*

> *generation, a royal priesthood, an holy nation, a peculiar people; that ye should shew forth the praises of him who hath called you out of darkness into his marvelous light:*

The prophet Obadiah put it this way:

> *[Oba 1:21 KJV] 21 And saviors shall come up on mount Zion to judge the mount of Esau; and the kingdom shall be the LORD'S.*

This verse speaks of saviors plural, so it isn't just Jesus. If you want to know who these saviors are pay attention to where they come from. They come from Zion. Hebrews 12 tells us that the Zion of God is the church:

> *[Heb 12:22-23 KJV] 22 But ye are come unto mount Sion, and unto the city of the living God, the heavenly Jerusalem, and to an innumerable company of angels, 23 To the general assembly and church of the firstborn, which are written in heaven, and to God the Judge of all, and to the spirits of just men made perfect,*

That means those saviors (other translations say "deliverers") are coming from the ranks of the church, and they are coming to judge the mount of Esau. Esau is religion. The mount of Esau is the sphere of the religious world that sold out true spiritual experience for dead form and lifeless doctrine. Judgment first comes to the house of God. If you ever stand up in your rights and entitlements the first task to accomplish is dealing with dead religion – in you first and then in the world. You have to put your inner Esau to death – who wants to sell out God's inheritance for a cheap facsimile that is only a fake knockoff of true spiritual reality.

Now when we talk about judgment, that isn't something that we want to throw a party and celebrate. It is a fearful thing to fall into the hands of a living God. Why would we seek out His judgments then? Because that is the "getting on" place to connect with His anointed process and climb Jacob's ladder to be one with the Father as Jesus was. Jacob saw this ladder, but he couldn't ascend. His only option was to pack up and go work for Laban, who changed his wages nine times. Are you tired of a Laban experience? You get somebody's book that promises if you do what they say or believe what they believe but by the time you get to the end of it they moved the goal post and you have to go to another conference, get another book or CD series. That's Laban, and we aren't interested in that. We don't want to see Jacob's ladder and turn our back so we embrace what that ladder brings because we want to move from the Spirit of the Fear of the Lord on the bottom rung to the top rung of the Spirit of the Lord Himself where we become one with Him and experience the full entitlements of salvation. This is more than a suggestion. We have walked it. We have in the mercy and grace of God experienced this in the last many years where everything we say and do has been as effective as if we said it or did it. This is reproducible and practicable if you are willing to:

1. Do what you see the Father do (John 5:19).
2. Have no opinion about the consequences (Matt. 7:1).
3. Relinquish the Outcome (John 12:24).

CONCLUSION:

In the book of Acts, when Ananias and his wife died before the Lord, the scripture says that great fear came upon all the people and no one dared to join the church:

> *[Act 5:5 KJV] 5 And Ananias hearing these words fell down, and gave up the ghost: and*

> *great fear came on all them that heard these things.*
>
> *[Act 5:11, 13 KJV] 11 And great fear came upon all the church, and upon as many as heard these things. ... 13 And of the rest durst no man join himself to them: but the people magnified them.*

Now how is it that no one dared to join with the church, but at the same time, the next verse tells us that hundreds were being added to the church every day?

> *[Act 5:14 KJV] 14 And believers were the more added to the Lord, multitudes both of men and women.)*

What is going on here? It's because the fear that came was not a natural fear; it was the Spirit of the Fear of the Lord that came down. God lowered His ladder and invited the people to ascend – to rise, rule, and reign. What happened next?

> *[Act 5:12 KJV] 12 And by the hands of the apostles were many signs and wonders wrought among the people; (and they were all with one accord in Solomon's porch.*

You see when Ananias and his wife died the Spirit of the Fear of the Lord came and immediately following that the Spirit of Knowledge came and imparted to the people and understanding of just what they were dealing with. God was not a God to be trifled with. What was the result? God check the ladder:

1. The Spirit of the Fear of the Lord
2. The Spirit of Knowledge
3. The Spirit of Might
4. The Spirit of Counsel
5. The Spirit of Understanding
6. The Spirit of Wisdom
7. The Spirit of the Lord (Himself)

This is how an OUTPOURING COMES! The Spirit of the Fear of the Lord came (Ananias died). Then the people reacted (they learned something about God; they didn't take into account – the Spirit of Knowledge). Then we know that the Spirit of Might is next and we find the apostles publically working many signs, miracles, and wonders. Where is the starting point? It is the Spirit of the Fear of the Lord. That is something you can do something about. You don't have to wait on someone to fall down dead. Even Jacob – heel grabbing, conniving, deceiving Jacob was able to position himself at the foot of that ladder that God showed him:

> *[Gen 28:12, 16-17 KJV] 12 And he dreamed, and behold a ladder set up on the earth, and the top of it reached to heaven: and behold the angels of God ascending and descending on it. ... 16 And Jacob awaked out of his sleep, and he said, Surely the LORD is in this place; and I knew [it] not. 17 And he was afraid, and said, how dreadful [is] this place! this [is] none other but the house of God, and this [is] the gate of heaven.*

What about you? It is going to happen one way or the other on the earth. We either place ourselves in God's process by design or by compulsion, but the Father says one way or the other you are coming to Me. What is the result:

Knowledge
Might
Counsel
Understanding
Wisdom

And lastly the Lord – being one with the Father walking in the entitlement of sons because your inner territory is now conquered, the giants are defeated, and the land of Milk and Honey lies before you as a gift of the Father to His loving children. Are you ready? Then let us begin with an embrace afresh and anew with the Spirit of the Fear of the Lord and go on from there.

Printed in Great Britain
by Amazon